# FROM
# STUDENT TO
# ENTREPRENEUR

## The steps I took
## and lessons I learned

**AILEEN GILANI** FOUNDER OF
THE LUXURY STUDENT

I AM SELF-
PUBLISHING

www.iamselfpublishing.com

**"**

# ACT LIKE THE CEO YOU'RE GOING TO BE...

## BY ME.

The Luxury Student is a private members club website available to students (and some bloggers) to enjoy the luxury life whilst they study at university. Here, students pay a monthly fee or a fixed membership fee (depending on the offer at the time) to experience a range of services listed online. These services and experiences offer our members the opportunity to continue their luxury lifestyle or taste the lifestyle that they wish to live. We offer students the opportunity to live like the CEO they are going to be!

# INTRODUCTION

My name is Aileen Gilani and by the time this autobiographical book (or quick read as I call it) is published, I shall be 26 years old.

I have always loved luxury. When I was 13, my goal in life was to look as 'preppy' as possible. I always wanted to look rich. I remember watching the MTV programme My Super Sweet 16. It was what I used to think was the dream. It followed 16-year-olds who had enough money and enough friends to plan very extravagant birthday parties. One of the things I remember was the amount of designer bags these 16-year-olds had. I wanted to be just like them.

Then came *The OC*. How I wanted to be just like Summer Roberts with her designer clothes. Then after that series ended, the famous series called *Gossip Girl*, which focused primarily on a rich group of teens enjoying a luxury life in Manhattan. Again, I wanted to be just like Blair Waldorf. I even tried to dress like her, but I didn't live such an extravagant life as her. Once, I bought a replica designer bag on holiday to Turkey, which cost me approx £30, hoping that no one would think it wasn't real. But one time the handle snapped and I decided that was the last time I would buy something that wasn't real and bad quality.

I was born in Sweden. We moved to Oldham (near Manchester) when I was four, and then, when I was six, we moved down south, towards London. My parents were hard-working business partners, running their own start-up. I could, therefore, see first-hand where the money was coming from, how it was earned, and more importantly, how they struggled to run their business. When it came to the summer holidays, every kid I knew would go abroad, or at least down to Cornwall. My sister and I knew that every summer was going to be spent sitting in the staff room of our parents' office, entertaining ourselves with books and colouring. Therefore, I was always so grateful for any treats that they were able to provide. I am still very grateful that my parents always tried hard to provide for us, even when they probably couldn't afford it.

So, the day I was able to walk into a store and buy my first designer handbag was amazing. I was celebrating my 18th birthday, finishing school and getting a university place. It was a triple celebration! I'm still quite old-fashioned as I like there to be an important occasion to purchase such things, like turning 30 or reaching some ultimate life goal, and even now only have a few, but each one represents a big turning point in my life.

My advice to you is don't buy fake bags, it's not worth it; especially when they break because the quality is so bad! And it's so embarrassing! Make sure you work hard, as I do, and earn enough to really enjoy the moment you buy that first luxury bag or accessory. As I grew older, I realised you should never be fake at anything or try to live in a way that makes you feel uncomfortable. I have seen many people feel pressured to buy the latest It Bag or experience something that other people are experiencing, but be true to yourself. Make sure you're Brand You, not Brand Fake You.

# FOREWORD

This book is for all the ambitious students, graduates, bloggers, and people who want to lead their own entrepreneurial lives. In fact, this book is for anyone who wants to hear my story (I'm young, so it's going to be short).

I started writing this two minutes after an interesting article was featured about my entrepreneurial journey. It had a cheeky headline – 'GDL dropout launches luxury private members club for London students seeking "the finer things in life"' – but it worked because it grabbed a lot of people's attention, which ultimately raised the brand awareness of my business. The article was about my journey to starting a business and the fact I had to drop out of university and take the opportunity to work on my business. But it wasn't the headline that I had a problem with, it was the comments that came with it. While some of the comments were full of positive feedback, I got my share of cruel criticism. Some people from this article called me 'dumb', 'stupid', 'vain', 'materialistic'. Others described my business as a 'waste of time' and said 'she's only doing well because she's living off rich people'. The worst described me as a 'failure' and an 'embarrassment'. Then there was the killer blow: 'she needs to get a life and find a proper job'.

I've had plenty of bad days as an entrepreneur. I've had people hang up on me, say that I'm a waste of time, people have ignored me, forgotten about meetings – I have had them all, even in the very early days of my business. I am here now, writing this book with a business that's thriving and, actually, now that I think of it, I'm a very successful dropout.

My aim is to share with you what I've learnt through all the stuff that's happened – the good and the bad, so you can prepare yourself for launching your start-up, especially if you're a student or a recent graduate. My branding tips should also allow you to take advantage of your personality strengths and show you ways in which you can promote yourself as a brand. My marketing tips can be adapted for any industry. Although my journey was largely digital, the fundamental steps are the same across all start-ups, and every start-up faces the same challenges, especially in the beginning when you are trying to gain traction and no one has heard of you. This is a step-by-step guide based on the experiences I have been through from the initial concept, starting my business, branding and all the ups and downs that came with it.

I hope it will show you that all the criticism out there cannot stop you from doing what you're passionate about and good at.

Although I believe there is no set way of starting a business, because every business is different, there are some fundamentals that you will be able to relate to and learn from whatever your start-up is. By the way, there is no data, no references from specialists or business strategists. This is just me telling you what I did right and what I did wrong, so you can get it right first time.

# THANK YOU

**F**or everyone's support, curiosity, patience and wisdom. And thank you to you, the reader, who wants to explore all options in life and ultimately wants to become a success! Don't give up!

## WWW.LUXURYSTUDENT.COM

# TIMELINE

### JUNE 2015

GRADUATED FROM
OXFORD BROOKES  UNIVERSITY

### AUGUST 2015

IDEA OF LUXURY STUDENT ON MY MIND

### SEPTEMBER 2015

ACCEPTANCE TO LAW SCHOOL
IN BLOOMSBURY

### JANUARY 2016

STARTED LUXURYSTUDENT.COM BLOG

### JUNE 2016

REGISTERED LUXURYSTUDENT.COM
AS A BUSINESS

### SEPTEMBER 2016

PAUSE LAW COURSE

### SEPTEMBER 2016

LUXURYSTUDENT.COM BLOGGER PLATFORM

### JULY 2016

PAUSE BLOGGER PLATFORM

### SEPTEMBER 2017

RELAUNCH LUXURYSTUDENT.COM
PRIVATE MEMBERS CLUB

### DECEMBER 2018

BOOK RELEASE

# CONTENTS

# FROM STUDENT
# TO ENTREPRENEUR

**"**

ONLY I CAN

CHANGE MY LIFE,

NO ONE CAN DO IT

FOR ME

**"**

CAROL BURNETT

# 01

# GRADUATED FROM UNI,
# NOW WHAT?

'm starting this chapter where it all began. I had just graduated from Oxford Brookes Hospital-ity School in June 2015, I loved my course and loved the university! I learnt lots, studied well and enjoyed the university life. But it took me longer to figure out what to do after finishing university. Maybe you can relate? I then thought of study-ing Law. I assumed a legal career would be more demanding than a hospitality one, but at least the pay was better, or so I thought back then. I found myself tossing and turning on what to do with life. These thoughts went around and around my head:

- *Should I just get a job?*

- *What job should I look for?*

- *Should I study further and get more qualifications? Would that help me get a better job?*

- *Should I start my own business? What would that be? Where do I start?*

- *How much money do I have in my savings?*

- *What are my friends doing? And why aren't they sharing their plans with me?*

The questions and subsequent panic attacks were endless. This anxiety is normal, and a lot of people go through this as they try to make one of the biggest moves of their lives. But you should know that plans can change, opportunities will come in, and yes, the struggle is real. We all go through it, just keep going. We don't admit to ourselves or even to our friends just how confusing life is at this tricky stage of graduation. At the same time, I was also considering starting my own business. I had no clue what the business would be, but it had always been at the back of my mind. To my surprise, soon after I graduated, I was offered a job at a marketing firm and funnily enough, on the same day, I received confirmation of my place at law school. Funny how things turn out in the end, as I had studied hospitality – not marketing or law. Sometimes the decisions you make lead to other opportunities that you never would have considered.

I took the place at law school, but it never really felt right. Something at the back of my mind felt that studying law was not the best choice, and that maybe I should have chosen the marketing role instead, as that probably would have given me more business knowledge and skills. But then again, would I have started the business that I run today if I wasn't surrounded by students? Who knows?

# LESSON 01

Always be flexible, this is a key part of the entrepreneurial mindset. Whatever you studied at school or at university, may not be the career you go for. This is because you choose a subject to study when you are a child, maybe 16 or 17, but your personal and professional development changes and you will experience so much in life, whether it is through travelling or work experience, that by the time you enter the world of work you are so different from the child who chose which subjects to study. So don't feel disappointed if you have this gut feeling that the course you chose when you were a teenager is not what you wish to do as a career.

**"**

THE FASTEST WAY TO KILL

SOMETHING SPECIAL,

IS TO COMPARE IT TO

SOMETHING ELSE.

**"**

CRAIG GROESCHEL

# 02

# GOOD GRADES OR BAD GRADES, WHICH MAKES YOU MORE SUCCESSFUL?

**W**ell, if I were to say that you should just chill and not worry about grades, that would be very irresponsible of me, because, at the end of the day, all industries are competitive and you need to stand out. Having said that, you don't need to be an A* student to run your own business. How you learn and absorb things is always going to be different from the person sitting next to you. I never did well in exams or anything academic – my best grade was a C. One time I even got an E grade, and my father thought it meant Excellent. However, I knew that when I worked on the job, I could pick up everything very quickly as I was very practical and hands-on. When I graduated from university, I received a 2:2, which, to be honest, for industries like law would only have made it more difficult for me when it came to job applications, but you never know. Does the 2:2 matter to me now? Of course not. I am running my own business and I am thriving.

Competing with your friends is so old school. Yes, it really is. The problem that I had at university and school – and actually still have any place where I am working with people – is comparison and competition. The amount of times I received messages from friends who meant well but made me feel awful, asking: what did you get in your assessment? What work experience do you have? What are you going to do with your life? etc. etc. These sorts of questions can only have two outcomes, ultimately they will make you feel really smug or really down. Please avoid this. In this journey, I decided that those horrid and awkward moments at university were not going to intimidate me when I was running my own business. I knew from the very start that I would always have competitors, or a business that does something similar, but I could approach that with a healthy attitude.

# LESSON 02

Make sure that you don't compare yourself to anyone. More importantly, do not compare your start-up with one that has been established for years. It will only make you feel behind at this early stage. Please look to brands and companies that inspire you, lift you up and show you what is possible, you don't want to be putting yourself down before you've even started.

**"**

IT DOES NOT MATTER

HOW SLOWLY YOU GO,

AS LONG AS YOU

DO NOT STOP.

**"**

CONFUCIUS

# 03

## DO I NEED WORK EXPERIENCE? SHOULD I WORK FULL-TIME BEFORE I START A BUSINESS?

Any work experience is good experience. I had previous experience at a hotel, as it was part of the course requirement to work in the industry. It wasn't a role with great authority – I was just an intern receptionist – but a smooth-running reception is vital to the smooth running of the hotel. I didn't feel like I had enough experience to start my own business at the time so this was a great opportunity for me.

At the very beginning, I was so nervous; the responsibility was terrifying. There was so much admin to do and bookings to deal with. Customer service was key. Consistency was key. 12-hour shifts were difficult, especially when I was in heels and literally standing all day. Smiling for 12 hours was the worst. All of which I really struggled with at the beginning.

Slowly, I got used to the pace and the intensity. I remember one time there was a mother who rang in quite a state and requested oatmeal or something that could help her daughter's upset stomach. It was 11:30 at night so you can imagine that it was difficult to find anything. The kitchen had closed and wouldn't reopen until breakfast time, but I remembered there was a small supermarket nearby on Bond Street Station, so I ran over there and luckily the store was open. At 12:15 in the morning I hand-delivered the oatmeal to the mother. She and her daughter were so shocked and so grateful. When I arrived for the following morning shift, they were waiting for me at reception. They gave me a Ladurée gift as a thank you. I knew that the ability to go the extra mile was crucial in this luxury hotel environment. I learnt a lot from working on reception. I met so many interesting guests (and some very rude ones), but most were very kind. It was the perfect experience for me, as it taught me a lot about customer needs and customer services, which is important for any business.

# LESSON 03

Find some work experience. This could be for a corporate brand, a start-up or even a family-run business. Don't worry if you can't find anything in the industry in which you want to work. The aim overall is that you need to find experience with businesses that have different business models. For example, you might want to choose one that sells memberships, one that provides services, one that sells products, one that is a local store, and even one that is part of a franchise. There is so much that you can learn from all these business models, and the skills you take from each one will feed into the bigger picture – your future business life. This is why all experiences are good. Yes, even the bad experiences are worth having as you just never know when it might add value to a situation you might find yourself in.

**"**

IF YOU CAN DREAM IT,

YOU CAN DO IT.

**"**

**WALT DISNEY**

# 04

# THAT'S SUCH A GOOD IDEA!

A t the age of 23, when I was six months into my law course, I thought of the idea of starting a blog one night when I couldn't get to sleep. It was one of those light-bulb moments. Before I went to bed, I did a last-minute check on social media and saw that some bloggers had posted about their recent purchase of the latest It Bag. Something clicked. I guess the concept of the blog began in the summer before

I even started the law course, so it had been in my mind for months before I had the confidence to actually start it.

In January of 2016, while on vacation in Tenerife, I finally started the blog. I was staying in a really beautiful hotel with a luxury spa, so it just triggered this confidence in me, that finally I had some interesting content to publish as my first blog. All I wanted at that time was to work on something fun and creative and write a few blogs when I was free from revising for my next law exam. We all have doubts, 'what-ifs' and 'maybe it's not the best idea', but give it a go – who knows where it might lead you.

# NOTES

.....................................................

.....................................................

.....................................................

.....................................................

.....................................................

.....................................................

.....................................................

# LESSON 04

**A**sk yourself how many conversations you have had with someone, or in a group, where you have said, 'That's such a good idea! We could do that!' This is exactly the energy you need when you first think of an idea. But not everyone starts off in this clichéd way. Sometimes it takes time to really picture the idea in your mind. It can be a conversation, a movie, or a very long and boring train journey. Sometimes it will take a few of these to connect to give you the foundations for your idea. Make sure you write a list of all your ideas – one day you will have the confidence to take action on one of them.

Sometimes, even the most obvious things in life will jump out at you and turn into a business idea. Sometimes the complaints you have or problems you experience will prompt you to think of a solution. The solution may already be there with a business that offers a service, but it may not resolve the problem completely, or it may not create the opportunity that you think it should create.

Be open-minded.

**"**

BY FAILING TO PREPARE,

YOU ARE PREPARING TO FAIL.

**"**

BENJAMIN FRANKLIN

# 05

## MARKET RESEARCH

Research. Such a dry word, I know. But it has to be done. However, my type of research wasn't about statistics or data or surveys (these are helpful though), it was simply cracking on with a concept – in this case, my blog. You can have all the statistics and data, but at the end of the day, you need to just start your business and introduce your concept to the world to really get an idea of what the reaction is like. That, fundamentally, is the most important thing. As a blogger, I knew that if people weren't engaging with, liking, following and reposting my content then my concept would fail. I conducted market research with both students and bloggers as I needed to see both perspectives. Their reaction and feedback were crucial to my growth. It is so important to see what the reaction to your product is like and welcome opportunities to learn from your audience.

I also had to test out the feedback from brands. As you know, bloggers aim to gain collaboration with and sponsorship from brands, so, ultimately, I wanted their attention as well. As I had called myself (or in this case, my blog) 'The Luxury Student', it was important for me to be associated with brands that were actually aligned with my target audience and preferred industry.

# NOTES

.......................................................................

.......................................................................

.......................................................................

.......................................................................

.......................................................................

.......................................................................

.......................................................................

.......................................................................

# LESSON 05

Get researching. When you do your research, whichever way you choose to do it, your goal is to find feedback from your future customers, brand partners and companies who will be working with you; that includes suppliers and anyone else you can think of. Having this knowledge now will put you in a great position. The best feedback I got was from brands that I actually started to work with. These brands will help you grow so that their business can grow with you too. I even asked them what they would do if they were in my position. Also, don't feel like you need to go for the best and most established brand first, my tactic was to try and find the smaller brands and start-up companies that were desperate for some exposure. So start small first and then this will help you build a great portfolio for you to approach more established brands.

**"**

THE PEOPLE WHO INFLUENCE

YOU ARE THE PEOPLE WHO

BELIEVE IN YOU.

**"**

HENRY DRUMMOND

# 06

## GET YOUR SUPPORT SYSTEM IN PLACE

I always used to think that my support and motivation should only come from my family and friends. Wrong. Your support system can include whoever you meet on this journey that will gladly give you feedback and enjoy helping you. I have had many people come into my life quite randomly who have helped me on this journey, some are my friends now and some are my mentors now, some are both!

You will meet brilliant people that you will need to welcome into your life and ask for their opinions. The fact that they don't know you personally will mean they will give you much better feedback than friends or family who might just tell you what they think you want to hear. I'm a total nerd for good karma. I totally believe that you need to be open to helping others because one way or another help will come back to you. Don't be a dry, competitive person who only thinks of yourself. Obviously, don't help your competitors, but you never know who you are helping and what sort of connections they have that they may end up recommending to you. I have helped many people who have either helped me directly or connected me with someone who has.

# NOTES

........................................................................

........................................................................

........................................................................

........................................................................

........................................................................

........................................................................

........................................................................

# LESSON 06

Connect with as many random people you can think of. Your best start point is connecting with your friends' parents. Why? They have already experienced a lot, met a lot of people and have probably got contact details of good companies that they have used and approved in the past. So connect with them, share your entrepreneurial story with them and maybe they'll know someone who can help you.

Once I got the confidence to reach out, I gained my support from people I met at events, on LinkedIn or Instagram, and even my friends' friends and family. Then I even went into restaurants whose branding I really liked and asked them who designed their logo, menu, branding, furniture, etc. I did this to find out which company they outsource these services to. It's a great way to research as well.

**"**

YOU CAN'T BUILD A

REPUTATION ON WHAT YOU

ARE GOING TO DO.

**"**

HENRY FORD

# 07

# THE REAL BLOGGER
# AND HOW TO BE PATIENT

Being a blogger in this 24/7 world now is a real struggle. It really is a full-time job to make it work. In my case, it was really difficult to juggle studying law with the fun of blogging. I obviously loved blogging and adding new content and setting up photoshoots, but it really was very time-consuming and, therefore, it affected my grades. It also affected my whole mindset and attitude towards having a career. I realised that blog-

ging can become someone's career. Some bloggers out there can make a lot more money than a
typical lawyer's salary. So, ultimately, I decided to
spend more time working on my blogging. I really
enjoyed it and it was really rewarding when brands
came back to me to offer products for free in return
for a blog or a post.

However, I didn't really blog for that long,
because at the back of my mind I knew I couldn't
juggle law and the blog forever. I wanted to figure
out a way in which the brand Luxury Student could
still grow, but without my time being consumed.
While I was trying to figure out what to do with this
blog, I knew that even at this stage I was personally
representing the brand, and this was really exciting.
I felt like a celebrity, like my personality and life was
interesting to people. But unfortunately, I wasn't
getting many followers. I knew that other bloggers
had thousands of followers so my first mistake was
not being patient. Eager for a shortcut, I stupidly
bought my followers. I paid a monthly fee and it

was OK for about 2 months until I realised I couldn't afford it. I stopped paying and then all of a sudden my followers dropped down from 1000 to just 100 followers.

I also tried to use this other service which sent messages and comments to other accounts to create an engagement in the hope that other accounts would respond and then follow my account. Again, this was stupid because this bot was sending messages to people who were not my target clients, from X-rated accounts to spam accounts. It was a waste of time and money. Once again, I had to stop what I was doing and just accept the fact that I had to be patient, develop my content and traditionally approach brands the normal way. There wasn't a blogger agency who could help me, or maybe there was, but I was just too nervous so I never joined. I sat down and started thinking of new ways to bring content and to develop my blog.

# LESSON 07

Consider all the different ways of reaching out to your target market. It is also very important to constantly develop your idea and don't be afraid to pull the plug on something that is not working as well as you had hoped. And please do not cheat your way to the top. This goes back to what I said about not buying fake bags – don't do it. Don't be fake. There is no point. It is not genuine and there is no way you can get away with it anymore. Be patient. Your followers, customers and clients will come in time.

**"**

ONE CAN CHOOSE TO GO

BACK TOWARD SAFETY

OR FORWARD TOWARD

GROWTH.

**"**

ABRAHAM MASLOW

# 08

## BE FLEXIBLE TO GROW

As I was researching different ideas for my blog, I was looking for events to attend that could teach me more about the blogging world. Whilst doing this, I saw that there were blogger community sites, forums and magazines. Soon I realised that there was potential for bloggers to all work together to create an information platform, which is in many ways like an online magazine, where each blogger can contribute an article/blog. I already knew that there were quite a few similar businesses already doing this in other areas, but I was very confident that my target market, luxury students, would appreciate the content from many different bloggers living their luxury student life.. I already knew that there were quite a few similar businesses already doing this in other areas, but I was very confident that my target market, luxury students, would appreciate the content from many different bloggers living their luxury student life. I realised I would need to create a platform that enabled more bloggers to enter, maybe even log in and write in the back end of the system to add their blog. This was a whole different project to work with but it was so exciting to think that I could run a blogger magazine or a new platform for thousands of bloggers to go into and promote themselves. I knew that I always wanted my brand to develop and be known worldwide, not everyone wants this so quickly but I craved it very quickly, especially in my market of students, bloggers, luxury and the digital world. Opening up to others was a great way to grow.

# NOTES

..........................................................................

..........................................................................

..........................................................................

..........................................................................

..........................................................................

..........................................................................

..........................................................................

..........................................................................

# LESSON 08

Think like an entrepreneur and brainstorm all the different ways in which your brand can expand, from the first product or service to anything that you can think of. Your brand will never just be one thing; brands need to develop to survive. Also, create yourself a timeline of how quickly you want to grow, as this will definitely affect your process of introducing new products or services, to make it more available to people. For example, there are many bloggers out there who started off writing about other brand's products and then went on to create their own personal brand products, from homeware and so much more.

**THE MOST EFFECTIVE WAY**

**TO DO IT, IS TO DO IT.**

**AMELIA EARHART**

# 09

# WHY AND WHEN TO REGISTER A BUSINESS

At 24, I registered this as a business the minute I decided it was going to create a blogger platform and I planned out all the different ways the money was going to come in. So my vision and business plan expanded into a platform that had different revenue streams, from advertising, blogger access, brand access, journalists, bloggers and so much more. I needed to think about and call The Luxury Student a business now, not just a casual blog.

In theory, this was also the best time to drop out of the law route because I had just finished my conversion course and the next phase would have been the Legal Practice Course, which I would start in September. So, in June 2016, I registered The Luxury Student Ltd. Registering your business is probably one of the most exciting tasks you will do because it will make it official, and suddenly you will go into this responsible mode. I only registered my business once I realised that there was potential in developing my concept into this bigger community platform. It was quite intimidating, and you do feel the pressure to crack on and start earning from day one, but realistically that is not going to happen. Registering is one of those admin tasks, which I strongly advise you do ASAP, so it's out of the way and you can start with developing your concept and preparing for your launch date.

# NOTES

......................................................................

......................................................................

......................................................................

......................................................................

......................................................................

......................................................................

......................................................................

......................................................................

# LESSON 9

know it's not that normal to register your business before you have a business plan confirmed, but in my case, it made sense. It's something that forces you to crack on. Use this as a way to really motivate you. Use all your resources and ask the relevant people the advice and guidance to register it properly. This is a big deal, therefore please make sure you that you celebrate this achievement. Crack on straight away with the business or activities you can do whilst you wait for the registration to go through, or your motivation will fade. As clichéd as it sounds, motivation is key.

**"**

THERE ARE ONLY TWO

MISTAKES ONE CAN MAKE

ALONG THE ROAD TO TRUTH;

NOT GOING ALL THE WAY,

AND NOT STARTING.

**BUDDHA**

# 10

## TIME TO WRITE A
## BUSINESS PLAN

N ow that I had dropped out of law school, I had to write a business plan. I couldn't just do this casually. It had to be structured and realistic. I had made a big commitment to it and I needed to take this seriously.

There are many platforms where you can buy what are effectively business plan templates. You pay a small amount and all you have to do is insert the details in each box and at the end it creates a snazzy business plan for you. These 'copy-and-paste' templates are great but you need to be careful not to make careless mistakes.

You must familiarise yourself with all the key terms of 'business plan talk'. Sometimes I don't understand why we have to use 'big words'. In my opinion, conversations like this need to be less intimidating. Nevertheless, not all dreams come true, so you must know what you're talking about. The best way is to google business plan words and terms and phrases.

Don't make the common mistake of thinking that your business plan is only about the numbers. Of course they are important, but it is also a chance for you to map everything out about your business, your values, your growth plans, even down to creating a customer service strategy. It's all fair and well to add all the customer service staff and costs, but have you actually written down the tasks and then steps needed to make having a great customer service team happen? By forcing yourself to go into such detail, you will really understand how much of everything you need (and get a better idea of costs). Go into as much detail as possible.

An HR strategy is also key. Hiring staff is not just about getting them to do the job and then paying them at the end of the month, it's also about retaining them so you don't have to keep hiring new people. So build a good HR strategy with employee benefits and incentives as well. These may all be costs you may not have thought about just yet, but it's better to think hard about absolutely everything now.

You also need to have a worst-case scenario for everything. The term 'forecast' reminds me of the British weather, when they say, 'Today it will be sunny and then it will rain and then hail and later you'll see a bit of fog and then lightning'. Business can go from one extreme to another, so make sure you have back-up plans in place that will keep you steady.

I also think that we tend to generalise our ideal customer in one target market when it's more useful to break that buyer persona down and go into more detail. My target market is students, but not all students. I'm interested in students who love the luxury industry. This is a much more defined group of customers and a much smaller group than the half a million students who start university each year.

We all tend to only look out for competitors in our own industry, but actually it is much bigger than that – you must look out for distractions. By this I mean whatever else your target customers might have been spending their money on. There are plenty of reasons why a potential member will not opt to subscribe, such as paying for upcoming festivals, saving money for upcoming sales or holidays they want to book. You have to really know your target customers and what times of year are good/bad for them. You must also find out all the reasons why they wouldn't become your customer or client, as this will help you figure out ways to overcome potential obstacles that could make them hesitant to purchase your product or service. In my case, some of my potential members don't join because they want to focus on their studies, or building their Instagram instead of joining another platform.

Please also note that these days, business plans are great, but usually you only need 12 to 15 slides if you are presenting it to anyone. Although it's always good to have the full detailed paper-work, nowadays business plans are often delivered in a presentation where you need to keep it precise and to the point. You can also research financials of your competitors (in my case, as I didn't have direct competitors, I looked up student websites and platforms for high street discounts). This can help you understand how quickly, or how slowly, they grew when they first started. There is more finan-cial information available than you think.

# LESSON 10

D o not be lazy or brief about business plans. At the end of the day, this business plan is for you to keep and use like a manual for your business. You need to keep updating it and tweaking it when you think it needs to be developed. Get people to read through it and allow them to give their opinion. Go to random business owners, some could even be in your family, ask them what their highest costs are and see if you can learn from their business. Remember to be realistic as well. When you're adding costs like wages, remember that there is also holiday pay, sick pay and even bank holidays to think of; every little bit will be a cost for you. In my case, I had to figure out how many Brand Ambassadors I needed and how much I could actually rely on them. I wanted students to be brand ambassadors, but then I didn't even consider that some students want to work specific hours and that they also have deadlines and exams and other reasons for not delivering results. You have to consider all scenarios when it comes to the running of your business.

**"**

YOU CREATE YOUR

OPPORTUNITIES BY ASKING

FOR THEM.

**"**

SHAKTI GAWAIN

# 11

# DO YOU NEED
# MAJOR INVESTMENT?

actually chose not to worry myself and spend too
much precious time finding an investor. Instead,
I chose to spend the £20k I was going to spend
on the next step of my law journey on my business.
I decided to give myself this much as it was a forgiv-
able investment if, worst-case scenario, it didn't go
well. It still gave me the pressure to make it work,
but I really didn't want to answer to anyone else at
this stage. When you get investment, you have to

give up a share of your business, which sometimes means double the decision making and double the pressure. I knew I couldn't deal with that at such an early stage.

I could have gone for a major investment but offering a share of my company was too much for me to worry about at such an early stage of my start-up. I also didn't have enough evidence to prove to any investors that this was actually going to work, I just had a gut feeling that it would.

My first investment was on a website, building the actual blogging platform. I hired web developers, which cost me approximately £3k. I then realised that I didn't need to spend so much money on it, as I found plenty of 'out of the box' website developers like Wix, Squarespace and Shopify where you can create your own business website and run it yourself. These options would have been much cheaper and would have allowed me so much more control.

We are so lucky now that we have nearly everything under our nose from websites to apps to platforms and libraries. Between your local library and the Internet, you have everything you need to just get on with things, whether researching a certain topic, checking out competition or even looking for a reliable person to do something for you.

It doesn't matter what type of business you are running, you must have a digital presence. Your brand will not grow by the traditional forms of word and mouth – it must be appealing to the eyes of the customer buying your product and service, the eyes of the potential customer researching about you and the customers who have visited your location or experienced your brand, which they will review and share with other people around them.

# LESSON 11

**D**on't feel intimidated by approaching investors. Know that you are the one with the great idea and great business. You need to feel as though it is you doing them a favour in allowing them to be part of your journey. Whether spending your own money or that of investors, make sure you really know the most cost-effective options, or you may regret it later when you find cheaper or better alternatives.

## A WORD ON INVESTORS

Now to a sensitive matter; I have had a lot of potential investors come to me with all their hope and glory (and money) and when conversations start to turn more personal it got slightly awkward. They didn't appreciate that I am currently engaged and obviously will get married at some point, and one day, fingers crossed, will have children. Being a woman who may want a family apparently does not sell well to some investors. It's frustrating, but it's a ruthless world out there. I have found that some investors will not like the fact that you might (or might not) get distracted from your business. In any of these situations, I personally walk away. My point here is that you must find an investor who will look beyond these very 'sexist and ageist' matters, and there are plenty of people who have succeeded in bringing up a family and actually living an entrepreneurial life. You need a good relationship with your investors, you have to be on the same page – if you get a bad feeling, walk away.

# NOTES

........................................................................

........................................................................

........................................................................

........................................................................

........................................................................

........................................................................

........................................................................

**"**

**COMING TOGETHER IS**

**THE BEGINNING; KEEPING**

**TOGETHER IS PROGRESS;**

**WORKING TOGETHER IS**

**SUCCESS.**

**"**

**EDWARD EVERETT HALE**

# 12

## BUILD CONNECTIONS

I knew at this point I was going to have to get more serious to make my blogging platform work. I was aware that I needed to find business mentors and business advisors that could help me figure out if this blogger platform idea could turn into a really successful business or not. This, to me, was key to getting it off the ground. Not for getting any investment, but for connecting with people who have had experience in business, luxury, marketing, sales, strategy, etc. All the elements that, as a young entrepreneur, you always need. I was never stubborn enough to think that I knew everything about anything, which is why going to events and going online to connect and network with individuals was necessary for me. This meant that I could receive feedback, mentors, business advisors. I am certain that half the people I am connected to do not realise just how crucial they are to my professional and personal development. I always say to people that networking is just another word for socialising. The only difference is going to different events, meeting different people from different ages and simply having a chat with them about what they do, what I do, finding a mutual interest and grabbing that business card. Don't be afraid to give them your business card at the very beginning. People are so used to this behaviour, it comes with the package and networking (socialising) experience. I buy mine from Moo, I like the quality and you can really play with the designs. I also made mine stand out by giving them a matt finish and rounded corners, which always made for great business card conversations.

# LESSON 12

**N**etwork! Go to as many networking events as possible. Not just the ones that you're interested in, but also the ones that you think are quite random. Every event allows you to meet new people. I have been to finance networking events, fashion, PR, local community events, even an Irish community business event. I am not Irish but I didn't care, I actually met really ambitious people, from investment bankers to CEOs of major companies, people that I am now connected to on LinkedIn. Also, before I forget, make sure you add a photo of your face onto your business card. It is so helpful for people receiving it, especially during events like these where there are a lot of people meeting each other for the first time. So stand out and make sure they remember you, even on a business card.

**"**

YOU CAN'T REALLY BE STRONG

UNTIL YOU SEE A FUNNY SIDE

OF THINGS.

**"**

KEN KESEY

# 13

## BRAVING EVENTS ON YOUR OWN

I found my mentors, but I also came across very interesting people in my time of networking and socialising. I was invited to the opening of Philipp Plein's store on Bond Street, just a few days before Christmas 2016. This, to me, was the most overwhelming situation I have ever been in. I had never gone to that type of event before. I had no idea how to dress, how to arrive. My mind was awash with questions:

Should I arrive via normal commute or with a high-class Uber Exec car?

Should I bring business cards? No. It's not that sort of networking, it's supposed to be fun.

Would I know or recognise anyone? That's OK, I have my mentor with me. Only on the day of the opening, my mentor emailed to say he was not going to make it, but that I should definitely go as it was a great opportunity. So I went.

Now, for those of you who are lucky enough to attend such events, you know that when they say to arrive at 6pm, they actually mean 7pm. I did not know this. I arrived at 5:45pm and was the first person there. This meant that I was actually able to view the collection before anyone else, which was amazing! The collection was, in my opinion, the definition of Cool Luxury, if that is even a title or phrase. Slowly, more people came, paparazzi also arrived, along with many other familiar faces, from famous socialites, entrepreneurs, singers, actors, and many others that I didn't recognise but I realised they were also very famous too.

I came across a number of men with great physiques, so I joined them and spoke one or two words to them as I viewed the collection. I only realised when I had adopted another loner like me, that they were professional footballers. I spoke to many people who had no idea who I was, but in some ways, I should have known who they were. Finally, the star of the show arrived and all of a sudden it got crowded. Mr Plein entered and it went crazy. It was a really intense and intimidating experience. By 9ish he left and everyone else left pretty much soon after. It was brilliant!

# LESSON 13

D o your research. Not the research I was talking about before, but the celebrity research. Know who the big players are in your field so that when you come across them at events you are clued up and can make a good impression. If you are invited to a special event, find out who the person hosting is connected with or seen with before you go. Become familiar with what their own branding is. And please, go to these events if you can, even if you are scared and are going on your own. I spoke to a famous entrepreneur's wife; I had no clue who she was married to.

**"**

IF THERE'S ANY MESSAGE TO

MY WORK, IT IS ULTIMATELY

THAT IT'S OK TO BE DIFFERENT.

**"**

JOHNNY DEPP

# 14

## RANDOM EVENTS

I decided to learn about starting a business, and find out what it was actually like. So I went onto the Eventbrite website, which I find is the best way to find out what events are going on in London. And by 'event', I mean networking events, luxury events, brand events, start-up events and more. You can search for any keyword and it immediately comes up with a list of related events close to you. So the first one I went to was actually a

Virgin start-up event called How to Make Business with Big Businesses. This was music to my ears. I thought 'yes, finally an event that I want to go to and can relate to'. So I went, with my new snazzy business cards (not with a business but with a blog). As I entered the venue, I saw that everyone had products or food or something edible in front of them. I wasn't sure exactly what was going on. I sat down next to a young lady who had the most interesting jams (made from everything from carrots to exotic fruits). I asked her why she had brought her products and she told me that this event was about making business with big businesses in the food industry. Then it finally clicked. Unfortunately, I hadn't read the description of the event exactly, so, embarrassingly, I had nothing to show.

There were buyers from Virgin Atlantic, Tesco, Waitrose and lots of other high-end food retailers. I knew that this was definitely not the right event to go to, nevertheless I stayed. I was really curious, and I actually learnt a lot from that event. Everyone had to do a pitch! I was so nervous, I had nothing to show them. But I was honest, I told them that I didn't have a food product, I had a platform for students to read about luxury food and luxury experiences. Believe it or not, they actually loved the idea, and somehow it grabbed more attention than all the other food entrepreneurs in the room. Being different from the rest was actually what made me interesting. I gave my business cards to all of these key buyers!

# LESSON 14

Go to business events, not just events that relate to only your topic, product or industry. Running a business in one industry is always going to have similarities with doing it in another industry, so go to them all! Go to the odd ones now and again to stand out from the crowd. It will certainly develop interest from the people around you and it will be a great insight and research opportunity for you as well. If your intention is to one day build an empire like Virgin, then you must research all industries. Networking in other industries is probably more satisfying because you can be a bit more relaxed, yet you never know when you might need these contacts.

**"**

I ALWAYS WISHED FOR THIS,

BUT IT'S ALMOST TURNING

INTO MORE OF A NIGHTMARE

THAN A DREAM.

**"**

EMINEM

# 15

## STAY FOCUSED

I had decided in the summer of 2016 to launch The Luxury Student Blogger Platform. How ambitious I was! Not so realistic though. And rather confusing. I had somewhat forgotten what the whole point of my brand was. I started as a passionate luxury blogger but had somehow become an empire builder. I ended up offering consultancy for student campaigns, managing bloggers, managing students who were bloggers too, adding blogs myself, creating a powerful social media account, adding advertising, running a website and pitching to brands. In theory, adding so many revenue streams was a great idea, but in practice it made it very confusing for people to understand what my business was really good at.

Looking back, I should have stayed focused on getting bloggers onto the platform to write their own blogs and growing this community of readers and writers. Then I would have built the credentials to attract advertisers and create blogger campaigns for luxury brands. Wouldn't that have made more sense? Again, it's not always about making money immediately, but growing your brand in other ways and raising awareness.

# NOTES

........................................................

........................................................

........................................................

........................................................

........................................................

........................................................

........................................................

........................................................

# LESSON 15

Stick to your plan or you will lose focus. Re-evaluate what you're doing, and tweak the plan if necessary. Don't be an egomaniac, narcissistic entrepreneur. Make sure you are not leading yourself to failure already. Write all your revenue streams down in your ongoing business plan. These can be explored later, but you need to make at least one service or product work really well before launching the rest. Don't make it difficult for yourself; be patient. Less is more. It is so obvious to me now that it wasn't a good idea to get distracted and spread myself so thinly, but when you're in the moment and somewhat stubborn and excited about everything, you don't realise it. Be realistic when you offer services or add-ons to your brand. Make sure that everyone is happy with your service. Don't have cash goals. It's not about cash grabs here.

**"**

I LOVE WHEN PEOPLE

UNDERESTIMATE ME AND

THEN BECOME PLEASANTLY

SURPRISED.

**"**

KIM KARDASHIAN

# 16

## THE POWER OF GOALS

Your goal for the first six months or year needs to be realistic. You need to make sure your goals are not just about cash, but also about the development of your brand. Success comes in all forms, just keep your eyes out for them. To give you an example, whilst I had many optimistic visions and goals for 2017 and 2018, I knew deep down that for a business and brand like mine to work (remembering that I would be starting from scratch because there was nothing like it on the market) my first goals should have been around building my brand, reputation and credentials, rather than trying to become a millionaire.

Many start-ups fall into the trap of solely focussing on financial goals because they are desperate to get their initial investment back. Remember that it usually takes between 1 to 3 years for a business to start generating a satisfying amount of profit, so be patient. I do believe that even though you may have used your money to invest into your business without return yet, you haven't lost. You have gained so much experience that it can only lead you to different opportunities. If you are losing hope and thinking of closing the business, make sure you have exhausted all your resources. Also, ask yourself whether you have really made the sacrifices you need to in order to make this work. How committed have you been? For example, instead of paying rent for a flat, do you really need to live there? Instead, live with your parents for a while, save the money and stress from your rent and invest that budget on something to grow your business.

It's your business, so you can change the concept at any time. You don't have to stick to the original idea. You have to be patient. After two years, I could finally see some improvement with my finances but it wasn't enough for me to prove that my idea was a good business to continue. I didn't want to give up, so I went back to the drawing board to think about how I could better reach my students, how I could make more money and how I could encourage loyalty among my customer base.

# LESSON 16

S it down and think about where you want to be after one month, two months, six months, and a year. I made the mistake of doing something that was beyond my expertise and capability when it was just me running around. Below are my guidelines, but they will need to be updated according to your business:

- ❑ *Month 1: set up your brand*
- ❑ *Month 2: build a lead up to a launch*
- ❑ *Month 6: have an interested audience*
- ❑ *Month 12: launch your product. Go live!*

In between months 6 to 12, you should have enough time to build up interest with potential customers and partners. However, it will also give you 6 months of research, to see if there is potential with your brand and to tweak things if necessary.

**"**

WHEN ONE DOOR IS CLOSED,

DON'T YOU KNOW,

ANOTHER IS OPEN.

**"**

BOB MARLEY

# 17

## YOUR WORKING ENVIRONMENT

I was really struggling, trying to figure out what I could do with this brand. I knew it had so much more potential. And I wasn't the type to give up either, or downgrade and make it into a hobby. I had arranged to catch up with my mentor at his private members' club. I thought this was going to be the most intimidating environment; a young girl, entering an exclusive crowd, where you can only be accepted if you are 'somebody'.

When I arrived, it was exactly how I thought it would be – a secret door. No advertising at all to make it clear for anyone. Anyone who had the right to access it knew where it was, and that was all that was needed. I entered and it blew me away. I couldn't believe that this type of luxury existed. It was like I had entered someone's very grand home at first, and it felt so enchanting and overwhelming at the same time. I said to myself, right then, that one day I would become a member.

We sat down and had our catch up, and in conversation I said that I needed to find a cost-effective place where I could work and network at the same time. In mid-conversation my mentor said, 'Why don't you join here? I can get you in, it will be absolutely fine'. I questioned this at first. I thought maybe it was just a sweet comment, and that it would never really happen.

It did make sense to join, instead of paying for a hot desk in a shared office. I needed to present myself in a luxury environment to represent the brand and show off the lifestyle that either my bloggers would dream of or that my clients could relate to. It felt like common sense. After a month, once my application and interview went through, I was accepted. This actually gave me my new idea of creating a private members club for younger people like me, students who would want to live the lifestyle I was now living.

# LESSON 17

**R**eally figure out what sort of impression you want to give people. Put yourself in the places and environments that will support your brand. Be wise with your money as well. Sometimes you don't need to go down the traditional office corporate route to get the jobs done. Work in a place that inspires you. It's better to be surrounded by your inspiration.

## MEETINGS - THE DOS AND DON'TS!

### CALENDAR INVITES

Use calendar invites. Sending an invite directly from your calendar means that the date and time, and even the confirmation, cannot get lost in the emails. Please send a formal invite so that both parties can accept it into their own calendars so it's in place and confirmed. It's an obvious one, but sometimes we forget that the smallest tasks can make your life so much easier.

## RELAXING VENUE

Always choose a venue that is comfortable for a meeting. Sometimes the high street cafes are not so suitable for meetings because it can be difficult to get a seat and then you have to wait in a queue to get your coffee. So choose a nice cafe or a restaurant that allows you to be served and taken care of. You don't need to go crazy on the fine dining, but a place that you can just talk and relax is crucial.

## DRESS RIGHT

I always think that meetings should be formal; formal language and formal clothing. Remember, first impressions count. I totally believe that at the beginning of your business journey, if there is just one thing you should make sure you get right, it is wearing a good outfit to your meetings. First impressions really are that important, and people will always remember what you wore. I understand that budget does have a huge impact on what you choose, but I don't think that is actually an excuse anymore, especially with sales coming in and out every week from different fashion labels. There have been plenty of meetings where I have been in heels and workwear but the other party has been wearing trainers. This is because that is what their business culture is like. In my point of view, I represent luxury brands and, more importantly, my own brand. So I need to look the type. I have never bought anything designer to wear at meetings because I never had the budget to do so, but I dressed professionally and, I believed, impressively and in a way that was representative of my business culture.

## TALK RIGHT

Your manner, tone and conversation skills all contribute to the first impression. Often my meetings start with up to half an hour of small talk – just chatting about my life and finding similarities or common ground with the other person. This makes the conversation flow very casually and naturally. Then I gradually move into the business conversation.

If you have arranged the meeting, then you need to lead the meeting, so make sure you have a set of small talk topics in your mind before you go. The other person will want to make sure you have some confidence and can talk freely. Lack of confidence does nothing for you.

## KNOW WHAT YOU WANT

Make sure that you have a goal for the meeting and have a back-up plan. Many meetings I have had have failed because I didn't know what I wanted out of them. I didn't know what the other party wanted either. I am also now at the stage where I feel comfortable to say no to meetings when I think there will be no beneficial outcome for my company. At your early stage, you need to meet as many people as possible and find out what they do and how it may work in the future when you're ready. Use these meetings as part of your research.

## BUSINESS CARDS

Always have a business card to give to them (make sure the details are correct). If you do not have one at that particular moment make sure you take their details, or if you already have them, make sure you offer to follow up with whichever form of communication they are most comfortable with.

## FOLLOW UP

Always follow up with an email after the meeting to say how nice it was to meet them, etc. Some people really stress about the perfect time to send this. My advice is don't worry about all this 'it needs to be over 24 hours from the meeting' nonsense. Email them the next morning, or even at the end of you day you met. There is nothing wrong with this. Always connect with them on LinkedIn after the meeting.

## BUY THE DRINKS

I am one of those overly generous people who, no matter what, will always aim to pay for the other person's drink. I totally believe that every little bit helps and that you must be the one to buy them the coffee. I think it's a nice gesture to buy them the latte or flat white. So when starting up a business you must have a budget for the wining and dining, or in this case the lattes and cappuccinos.

# NOTES

........................................................................

........................................................................

........................................................................

........................................................................

........................................................................

........................................................................

........................................................................

........................................................................

**"**

SUCCESS IS ABOUT
DEDICATION. YOU MAY NOT
BE WHERE YOU WANT TO BE
OR DO WHAT YOU WANT TO
DO WHEN YOU'RE ON THE
JOURNEY. BUT YOU'VE GOT TO
BE WILLING TO HAVE VISION
AND  FORESIGHT THAT LEADS
YOU TO AN INCREDIBLE END.

USHER

# 18

## DON'T GET DISHEARTENED IF OTHERS CAN'T SEE YOUR VISIONS

t took me the majority of 2017 to decide to target the student market as a bigger platform than just the blog. It was straight after being accepted to the club that I realised that there wasn't one for students in these exclusive areas. I saw the opportunity for bringing the students that followed my blog platform into these exclusive members' clubs. It seemed like a perfect match.

So the first step was to discuss my idea with the club I was part of. My pitch to them was to offer my members the opportunity to use the facilities at the club in a small way. I wasn't sure if the club would grant them full access but a day or two a month seemed reasonable. I dreamed of my members purchasing a joint membership giving them access to both my online club and this physical London club. They actually really liked the idea, and we even discussed doing a taster day for my members. They were a bit nervous about having such young members but equally excited that should my members join they would continue to use their facilities even after graduating. The only problem was that they wouldn't accept anyone under 21 years old. The main cause for this decision was due to their previous horrendous experience of hosting a 21st birthday party. It turned out to be a crazy night with many people getting drunk and throwing up everywhere. So, naturally, they did not want a repeat at future events. So my idea of partnering with them came to a halt. But it meant there was interest. I called other clubs and venues and they were very happy to welcome them.

Another obstacle was trying to prove to these clubs that not all students were on a budget. The students that I was targeting were not interested in cheap drinks, but more quality services and memorable experiences. It was frustrating at times to always have to explain this to brand owners or store managers or venue directors. I knew from my blogging experience that there were so many wealthy and trendy students, so it was peculiar to see that no service provider or business seemed interested or even aware of this cash-rich demographic. What a waste of a potential opportunity. This actually made me even more driven. Even while I was walking through the streets of London, I could see that there were so many young individuals going to shops and buying an endless amount of clothes. Were these people invisible to the companies I was trying to work with? Why didn't any of the luxury brands have a connection with this demographic? No relationship between students and luxury brands existed, beyond maybe the odd student discount. This was my new struggle.

# NOTES

........................................................................

........................................................................

........................................................................

........................................................................

........................................................................

........................................................................

........................................................................

........................................................................

# LESSON 18

n business, there is no good luck or bad luck. You just get people saying yes and people saying no. So don't take it personally. Your idea may be truly the best one out there, but people may not have the budget or the permission or even the vision to move forward with you. Whatever happens, make sure you start the relationship positively and end the relationship positively. That way you can always approach them again in the future. So thank them for their time or consideration, in six months' time, go back to them again and share with them your updates and development, so they can see how far you've come since they stupidly said no.

**"**

EVEN IF YOU FALL ON YOUR

FACE,  YOU'RE STILL MOVING

FORWARD.

**"**

VICTOR KIAM

# 19

## BACK TO SQUARE ONE

Don't be afraid to go back to the drawing boards. Although building my blogging platform had originally been my goal, I realised there was something more exciting to work on. To suddenly realise that I could create a whole new trend and new way of thinking to me was so thrilling.

When I finally decided to basically start over with a whole new idea for the business, it felt like I needed to approach brands in a very different way now and under different goals. In the very beginning, it was just me representing the brand. Then it became myself representing a blogger platform to sell advertising, now it was me going to brands and getting them on board to offer benefits and perks for my student members. The game was different this time. It was even harder, but also more exciting.

Many of these brands strongly believed that all students are on a budget and therefore it is a wasted effort. Some seemed quite interested but it was difficult for them to add such projects to their yearly goals because they had never done anything like it before. It was very difficult to share the same visions. This was frustrating, but it was also very rewarding when I could see people reacting to this idea like it was one of those key light-bulb moments. Suddenly, they got it. I could offer them direct access to a demographic they weren't currently targeting but who had both the money and the desire to spend with their brand, all they had to do in return were a few perks and offers – I wasn't even asking them for ad spend. Also, if they could get my members interested in buying their products at such a young age, they could potentially be customers for decades.

When the brands were interested, they wanted to know specific details about my members and students in general, as some of them still struggled with the concept that students could be willing to spend big money on their brand. They wanted data that just didn't exist. There wasn't much market research, data, or any business that had done anything like this before. So, for that reason, my proposition was rejected many times.

However, I kept on pitching as I needed lots of luxury experience providers that would really appeal to my target audience – everything from fashion labels to household services. I spoke to fashion stylists, PAs, luxury chauffeurs, salons, anyone that could help create a luxury lifestyle for my members. It was vital to get a number of services on board to be appealing enough for students to pay to become my members.

I wanted students who loved luxury and were happy to spend on luxury to join my membership. In order to do this, I needed to make this membership site the only site that caters for these types of students. I needed to make it current and trendy for them as well. It had to be sophisticated enough, but also young enough to appeal to my market. Everyone has their own definition of luxury and what they think trendy is, but my goal was to make it appealing to the super wealthy students who have the budget for living such a luxury life. This was much harder than you might think.

The aim was to create an application form where students would need to apply before being accepted or declined entry to the membership. This would give it an exclusivity. It would be silly to say that I wasn't targeting those 1% high net worth students, but at the same time, I didn't want to make it even more niche than it already was. I never wanted it to be just 'for the rich kids' because I wanted my business to grow, so it was important not to intimidate people.

# LESSON 19

When you start a business, no one tells you that every day you are practically relaunching your business. Because every day you learn something new or something goes wrong, so you learn and make changes and do things differently. You might have some really big things go wrong, so wrong you have to completely overhaul your business. If this happens, you should not feel like this is a failure. I turn the word 'failure' into 'relaunch' because that's what I believe it should be treated as. The change or relaunch of your business needs to be seen as another exciting opportunity. If this happens, stay positive and use this time to go all the way back to the drawing board and even go back to all your old contact books or LinkedIn to let people know about your new and exciting relaunch; you never know, it might win the client or project you had aimed for before.

**"**

**KNOW YOUR WORTH!**

**PEOPLE ALWAYS ACT LIKE**

**THEY'RE DOING MORE FOR YOU**

**THAN YOU'RE DOING FOR THEM.**

**"**

**KANYE WEST**

# 20

## BE CAREFUL OF
## WORKING FOR FREE

here are two sides to every deal. What I needed was for luxury brands to give my potential members something special – either an offer or exclusive discount or maybe even a special event. It was obviously very ambitious but that's what my target was. The only catch was that for most brands, I didn't have the confidence to push the negotiation and ask for commission or a cut or anything that could reward me or give me an alternative incentive. I was bringing customers to them, after all and so I should have asked for something in return. Sometimes you just live and you learn. I wish I could say I am totally confident in negotiations now, but I am better.

I was so desperate for any collaboration with brands to make sure that I was still on target for my website relaunch. It was hard work, and to grab their attention I felt I had to offer the collaboration for free. This is a confusing one. It's confusing because, as a start-up, partnerships and collaborations are attractive as they can give you great exposure, but it's obviously better to get some kind of financial return too. If you are going to go into these freebie deals, be careful how many of them you commit to.

I am someone who easily falls into the trap of giving too much for free. However, the truth is, helping brands or smaller businesses is only a good thing. I have helped many in the name of collaboration and it only strengthened my credentials and portfolio, which was my aim after failing the first and second time. I used to be the biggest pushover when it came to pretty much anything. I desperately want people to like me and want to do business with me. However, there is a thin line between you wanting someone to do business with you (maybe even for no cost) and the other party actually taking advantage of you because you're being too soft or easy. When I compared my business to others I realised that they were managing to monetise things that I tended to do for free to make a good impression. That was so wrong. Something had to change.

Now brands pay to be part of The Luxury Brand Partnership. I have earnt the right to charge them. I select only the best and offer them the opportunity to be part of my collection. Although I knew that some brands would decide not to be part of the partnership anymore, because now they have to pay, it was a step I needed to take – I had to start charging. People love free exposure and free partnerships, but now that we had the value and asked them to pay, they were no longer interested. Maybe I should have charged them from the very beginning, but would that have lost me the initial much-needed business? Maybe. Who knows? It's all learning curves.

# NOTES

......................................................................

......................................................................

......................................................................

......................................................................

......................................................................

......................................................................

......................................................................

......................................................................

# LESSON 20

You shouldn't be afraid to ask for money in return for your work. It's easy to make the mistake of doing something for free. You need to make sure you set some guidelines and realistic expectations for yourself and the other party. When finding the brands or companies you want to collaborate with, make sure that they invest in you as much as you invest in them. Make sure that you ask them how you can grow with them, so they can visualise your future relationship as well. Be really straight about it. Talk to them about it and ask for their opinion. Put them in a position that makes them feel it is a great opportunity that they cannot turn down.

Then, as your brand and business grows, you have every right to say no if you don't get a formal agreement with financial incentives on both sides. The value of your time increases and the value of your business also increases. So why do anything for free anymore? This may be a very obvious question, but when you're running your business, you need to be careful of falling into the trap of offering too much free opportunity. You will always have the what ifs of whether you should have charged someone lower or higher or not at all, but let that part go. Move on.

# NOTES

........................................................................

........................................................................

........................................................................

........................................................................

........................................................................

........................................................................

........................................................................

........................................................................

**"**

IT'S ALL TO DO WITH THE

TRAINING: YOU CAN DO A LOT

IF YOU'RE PROPERLY TRAINED.

**"**

QUEEN ELIZABETH II

# 21

## SKILL UP!

If you find yourself really struggling to move forward with your business in making sales or partnerships, figure out why that is by looking into every step you make when dealing with a customer or client. In my case, I found that I was pretty good at selling myself on email, but when it came to having a conversation or meeting, I was unable to finalise or close the deal.

This was something to do with not being confident to negotiate. In person, I had no clue how to negotiate or read people. I didn't know how to turn conversations around if the other party was struggling to make a decision. I never had a plan A, let alone a plan B or C!

This step is vital in my opinion, and this is what I call 'self-investing'. This has nothing to do with investing in your actual business, per se, it's investing in your skillset. I decided that I needed to go to a negotiation course run by Activia. The course I chose was called Basic Principles of Better Negotiation (there are advanced levels as well). This 1-day course was exactly what I needed at the time. I came out with more confidence, more insight into people's behaviour and more understanding of how to read facial expressions and body language.

I also took a web coding course which was run by General Assembly in London, this gave me a chance to actually learn a couple of coding techniques for my own website. I had decided not to use two of my original developers anymore. Instead, I wanted to give Squarespace and Wix a go. The course was brilliant, but I wanted to know a bit more, in case I needed to develop my website further.

This 2-day course, which I thought was quite intense, was so helpful and it was nice to learn something new. However, I knew, after the course, that this was something I really couldn't do on my own. I would still have to hire in a developer, but now I knew so much more about the terms and would be able to brief them better. It's also good to know when you need a web developer, as I thought I needed one immediately but actually I have not used one as of yet.

# LESSON 21

Think about where you need to improve and what courses would be useful to go on. You may be able to find some free ones, but if not it's worth investing in things that will help you drive your business forward. So go to more classes, go to more training courses, keep learning, because it will be useful for you no matter what.

**"**

THE WAY A TEAM PLAYS

AS A WHOLE DETERMINES

ITS SUCCESS.

YOU MAY HAVE THE GREATEST

BUNCH OF INDIVIDUAL STARS

IN THE WORLD, BUT IF THEY

DON'T PLAY TOGETHER,

THE CLUB WON'T BE

WORTH A DIME.

**BABE RUTH**

# 22

## OUTSOURCING VS DIY

So many of my bad decisions have been awarded the 'Well, it was a learning curve' statement. The problem with this is that some of my learning curves have been thousands of pounds' worth. I made a mistake at the very beginning of relying on too many opinions and too many little outsourced services. With so many parties involved, managing everything, even when it was outsourced, got difficult. I particularly regret outsourcing the running of my website, as this caused too many issues and too many delays in the smooth running of my business. I would have been better off doing some of this myself. I had to stop everything and just say 'no'. It's OK to say, 'No, thank you'. Or even in your own words, say 'You're fired!'. It may sound scary, but it's your company and you can't have people slowing you down or wasting resources, especially if it's something you don't really need to have.

There will be many businesses that will naturally find you and pitch to you their services to help your business run more smoothly. Really consider whether you need a marketing specialist or a web specialist or a brand specialist when you may be able to do it all yourself with a little bit of research and time management.

However, there were some skilled tasks I was happy to delegate to someone else. In my case, I decided that most of my own investment into the business was going to go towards PR. This was because I needed to build awareness of my brand.

I knew that if I tried to do it myself it was going to take much longer and, knowing what I'm like, I would make a lot of mistakes before getting it right. I knew that I needed a proper team to push my brand out there and bring it to life as a national topic, and I was happy to pay for that.

I decided that my time was precious and that it should be consumed by sales, meeting people or creating partnerships, so although I no longer wanted to outsource little elements like web management, I could see the value in hiring a PR agency to create a campaign for me. There are many articles out there that encourage you to work on your own PR and other elements of the business, but from my own experience I knew that if I were to work on my own PR (which of course would have been much cheaper than paying an agency) it would mean that a lot of my time would be spent on creating press releases, making sure the grammar and style was good, finding the right journalist or editor, sending feature pitches, chasing up journalists, and so on. This is really time-consuming, especially when you don't know what you're doing or have the contacts. So my first decision was to invest in a good PR agency that understood my intentions, knew how to work outside the box and get the job done. This freed up my time to concentrate on sales, because I knew that the PR was under control.

# NOTES

........................................................................

........................................................................

........................................................................

........................................................................

........................................................................

........................................................................

........................................................................

........................................................................

# LESSON 22

Make sure you know when you need help and specifically what for. When we have too many tasks to do in our day, we are unable to fully complete every task. Make sure that you are honest with yourself about your time and budget. You have a lot of responsibility, but sometimes giving it to people who are experts at it, is going to allow you to work on the elements that you are strongest at. But do not get carried away and rely on help too much, as there will be times when you have to let go of assistance or delegating to other people. This could be when funding runs low or you may have even reached a point where you can now do it yourself. So do not feel obliged to stick to the same people or the same amount of help. Review things and assess what value the outsourcing company is really bringing to your business.

**"**

A HAPPY LIFE IS ONE SPENT

LEARNING, EARNING AND

YEARNING.

**"**

LILLIAN GISH

# 23

## LISTEN TO YOUR CUSTOMERS OR YOU'LL LOSE THEM

So the day came in September 2017, I was finally able to call my business The Luxury Student Private Members Club. It was the most exciting thing happening in my life. The nerves were high, the expectations were high, so many exciting things were about to happen. My first pitch was to a few universities (I could only afford to go to a few because universities charge a pretty hefty fee to have a table at their freshers' week fair).

The first one I went to was at a London fashion school. I went in there, not really knowing how to approach the students. In order for me to bring all the promotional material to the venue, I had resorted to using a few of my big, yellow Selfridges bags, and of course, once I emptied everything and set up my table, I moved them onto the floor.

People came to my stall and looked straight at those yellow bags. They must have thought that I was going to offer them something in the bag, so they came towards me to talk to me. Luckily, I am quite an approachable person and fairly good at selling, so I ended up with 20 new members signed up that day. You could call these my founding members. There were plenty of issues on the day, with far too many technical errors, but I powered through and made it happen.

But then, after a few weeks, people started complaining and cancelling their memberships. I knew that I needed to step up my game from customer service to concierge service. I needed to provide better communication and offer simple luxury perks. I became really insecure about my business. What I had thought would be great benefits for my members actually turned out to be quite useless ones for the students that signed up. I decided that I needed to, in some way, go back a step and really think of the strategy and the customer journey. I wanted desperately for something like this to work, it just had to work, or else. God only knew how I would deal with another failure. But in some ways, I had already failed and I needed to make it right. I spent the next few months really engaging with my target market, making even more effort to the newest members and making loyalty and recommendation the key to the success of my business.

# LESSON 23

When you launch your business, one of the crucial steps is to make sure you figure out all the little obstacles that can come your way. Make sure you know how to resolve problems, how to retain your new customers or clients and how to give them the best impression. Once again, you must make your first product or service work well and you must be patient as well. Allow the customer or client to feel like they are part of your brand as well. Listen to your customers, what you thought would be attractive or important to them may not actually be, there may be another element that you haven't thought of. Listen to all the feedback, even the complaints.

**"**

EXPECTATION IS THE MOTHER

OF ALL FRUSTRATION.

**"**

ANTONIO BANDERAS

## 24

# FRUSTRATION IS KEY!

I believe that frustration is key to the success of a business. My success came when I began sending pitch emails to luxury brands to partner with me. Even after relaunching in September 2017, I was still fighting for new partnerships and struggling to come up with new ideas to both partner luxury brands and keep my members happy and excited. My end goal at that time was to partner with as many brands as possible and to use this as leverage for bigger brands and also to create success stories for my PR. It is much harder than you realise. These brands receive so many emails, and I was often put at the bottom of the pile. Or worse, classed as spam.

One day in early 2018 I just had enough of waiting for someone to respond to my emails. I decided to walk into the luxury stores on Sloane Street and introduce myself in person. There was one brand in particular, which I didn't really think would work with our target market, so my first instinct was to practice with this store and see how the conversation went. To my shock, it was actually a success and they wanted to exchange business cards. What a relief!

So, feeling confident, I went straight into the next one and the next. And what do you know, I soon had business cards from all of my favourite luxury brands in my hand. It was like I had won the lottery! I went straight home, opened a bottle of champagne with my fiance and began calling all the people who I knew would be proud of me.

My partnership with these stores wasn't formal. We didn't sign contracts; it was an agreement that my members were welcomed at their store. In addition to that, some of the store managers offered to create special events for us to bring our members to their stores.

When I look back now, I should have made it clear to these stores that I should get a commission from any sales made by members. I think it is only right and fair to do this in general, but at the time, all I wanted and needed was brands to get on board and offer something valuable to my members. I never wanted any of the store managers to go back to head office and discuss it there, as I knew then it would take months to finally get the green light. Today, we have great relationships with our luxury brand stores because I have worked hard to establish these trusting relationships. This means I am in a much better position to work with them for future projects and ask for more.

# LESSON 24

I think you know what this lesson is going to be – sometimes you just have to power walk to your goal. If you trust in what you're doing, people will follow. If you are fed up of waiting to hear back from people, do something about it. Sometimes it is vital to make that dramatic entrance or find the number of the CEO and get them to listen to you. Be open to communicating in unconventional ways. Go with the flow and grab them, even if you end up working together for free. Go find them, go to events that you know they will attend, or stand outside their offices if you have to.

**"**

YOU HAVE ENEMIES? GOOD.

THAT MEANS YOU'VE STOOD

UP FOR SOMETHING

SOMETIME IN YOUR LIFE.

**"**

WINSTON CHURCHILL

# 25

# DEALING WITH HATERS

The most shocking episode of my business start-up was the moment I realised my membership sign-ups were too good to be true. Typical. One minute it's too bad; one minute it's too good. I was invited to a university in London to present The Luxury Student at their freshers' week. It was a great opportunity for me because this was the perfect place to grab those students. Well, I thought it was the perfect place. The students who found my membership interesting took some of my promotional material and considered joining. There was a group of young male students who came towards me, excited that they could join a members club like mine and gain all this exclusive access to brands and experiences. These guys were very wealthy and very intimidated by each other. As one said he would join, another said, 'I will only join if you join'. In my head I could picture the dollar signs, knowing that I would leave this freshers' week fair with a few thousand pounds in my pocket. Well, that dream crashed very quickly. They said that they wanted to pay in cash and needed to go back outside to the cash machine. I said that was absolutely fine and I looked forward to making them my members, but about half an hour later I could see them wandering in the hall and avoiding my area completely. I decided that I shouldn't take it personally and it didn't matter if they didn't join. The shock was what came after. One of the young men came back, stood close to my stall and stared at me for a good ten minutes. A few other people came towards my stall and I started pitching to them as normal. At the same time, one of the young men that was in the group came in between the people, took a couple of my leaflets and ripped them in front of me, saying that I was a scam! He told me that he didn't think I had any partnerships with these brands and that there was nothing about me online so I must be a scam.

My heart sank, then it started beating so fast I felt sick. I could feel my whole face burning. The other students also looked at me in horror. I quickly reassured them that this was not the case and that it was a registered business with support from all the luxury brands on the website. The troublemaker walked away. I wished there was a black hole that I could sink to, to start crying. I wanted to jump right in because I felt so humiliated. My mind was over-thinking in every single way.

Ten minutes later, I became really angry that someone so unaware of running a business, so rude and disrespectful of new businesses and new concepts, could get away with saying something like this. So I called the security guards and we soon got him escorted out of the premises. Apparently, he apologised to security but he never came to me to apologise, which I guess just shows how stupid he was. I got back home, immediately called my PR agency, cried to them, and said we needed to work on this, so that no one would ever consider my business a scam. I relied on a good reputation. To think that after all the hard work of creating my innovative business, that was so cool and with such a great USP, that someone would say this! To him, my business was too good to be true! What a nightmare! When I have explained this to other people, a lot of them say it was simply bad luck and a very extreme situation, but truth is, when you run your own start-up, it only takes one bad comment to make you panic. It feels personal and it's very hard not to get upset.

# NOTES

..........................................................................

..........................................................................

..........................................................................

..........................................................................

..........................................................................

..........................................................................

..........................................................................

..........................................................................

# LESSON 25

**H**aters gonna hate! This follows on from the first rant at the beginning of this book. You will always have people who are not open-minded and lack vision and faith. So keep going, don't bother getting angry or upset like me – I cried for hours! For every 10 negative comments, you're going to get the most wonderful, random messages from people around the world, wishing you well and giving you the positive vibe that you deserve.

When the negativity comes, don't take it too personally. There will always be people who will hate your brand. People will complain in their own way, it's not always going to be via email or letter, some people will post a video about you, send social media comment back to you or do it to you in person. They may have absolutely no grounds at all. I now have a much thicker skin. Now I bring a team with me to these events, so I'm not on my own. I will always stand my ground to defend my brand. I laugh at that memory now.

**"**

MEDITATION, MORE THAN

ANYTHING IN MY LIFE, WAS

THE BIGGEST INGREDIENT OF

WHATEVER SUCCESS I'VE HAD.

**"**

RAY DALIO

# 26

## MEDITATION

I have cried many times, especially during events like the one mentioned in the previous chapter, or just from being tired and mentally drained. I realised the stress of the business was making me slow down and I had such a lack of confidence. Meditation, it's not uncool anymore, so just embrace it. I find that it gives me energy and helps me calm down when running my business becomes too stressful. I struggled a lot to keep a good routine and a healthy lifestyle. Please make sure you give yourself breaks. Me sending emails at 11pm made no difference to the decision making of the receiver, as no one was going to answer me that late because they have a life. So make sure you have one too! A frazzled brain is a useless brain. Find something that calms you down like running, dancing or yoga. Schedule it in like you would any other important meeting. I've done so many things just to get myself out of the flat or out of the office, from taking up ballet to booking cinema trips or taking random classes. And it worked!

# NOTES

......................................................................

......................................................................

......................................................................

......................................................................

......................................................................

......................................................................

......................................................................

......................................................................

# LESSON 26

Please be careful of falling into the availability trap. If you say, 'I'm available all the time, and on my phone and on WhatsApp and on other platforms' people will start to expect this as normal. Ultimately, this is not how you should do business because it will not allow you to have a break. People will expect you to be there for them 24/7 and will be disappointed when you are busy. People also want to feel like your time is valuable. It will make them grateful for your time. Make sure that you keep some of your time for you, so you can be fresh and energised when you get back to work. I use an app called Calm which is great for meditation. I listen to it every night and sometimes I listen to it during the day as I drink my latte in my break.

**"**

NEVER WORRY ABOUT BAD

PRESS: ALL THAT MATTERS IS

IF THEY SPELL YOUR

NAME RIGHT.

**"**

KATE HUDSON

## 27

# GOING VIRAL

In a week in April 2018, the PR agency and I had decided to approach more digital/online magazines that were becoming trendy with our target market. Before, we had only approached other bloggers for reviews, and although this was great, it was not quite enough to get our name out there. So we decided to give Refinery29 a go. I always, always read their articles because it was female-driven, with female voices writing on topics I could relate to. I was so excited to hear they were happy to publish an article about me and my brand. It came out on the Friday, which was perfect for all the weekend readers. On Monday, I couldn't believe that The Independent also wanted to feature us. Questions were being sent to me to answer, which the PR agency checked for embarrassing grammar and spelling mistakes. Then, to my surprise, on Monday afternoon, they actually published the article. I remember walking past Selfridges and calling my mum and dad.

I shared both articles with as many people as I could. Then to my shock, Business Insider approached me, and also published an article, then the Daily Mail published one the following Saturday! It was the craziest week of my life. I had never imagined it to just happen like that! The interviews, the phone calls, the WhatsApp messages and the LinkedIn messages just kept coming!

# NOTES

........................................................

........................................................

........................................................

........................................................

........................................................

........................................................

........................................................

........................................................

# LESSON 27

One thing I have learnt about PR is that you have to be patient, and you have to really understand who your readers are. Who are you trying to target? For me, it was luxury students. So all online platforms that students would go to were worth pitching our story to. If, for example, your target market is women in their 50s then you would obviously target the publications and journalists that write for that audience. And lastly, is it brand exposure you want or sales? Be careful and realistic when putting yourself out there. My amazing brand exposure didn't lead to thousands of new members, it led to readers understanding and trusting what my business was all about. It also gave our new potential partners confidence, as when they researched us they could see all these articles from serious publications and tell we were legit. Another point, people's reaction to the articles may not be what you are looking for, so make sure you have a thick skin and be prepared for stupid people commenting nasty things about you. Dealing with negative comments is normal in running a business. Just keep going and look at the bigger picture. Always look at the bigger picture.

# NOTES

........................................................

........................................................

........................................................

........................................................

........................................................

........................................................

........................................................

........................................................

**"**

WHOEVER IS CARELESS WITH

THE TRUTH IN SMALL MATTERS

CANNOT BE TRUSTED WITH

IMPORTANT MATTERS.

**"**

ALBERT EINSTEIN

# 28

## READ BETWEEN
## THEIR LINES

In the midst of receiving my week of viral press, so many people came into my life, left, right and centre, from all different brands and countries. It was, to say the least, flattering, and it made me feel like I had 'made it'. The definition of 'made it' for me was that I finally had a standing, a foundation, an authority over this market and over the luxury brands, and in general. For a month, I said yes to everything, and this time round it wasn't me who was pitching to companies, it was the other way round. When a business approaches you and offers to partner or to work with you in some capacity, they must have a good reason. There will always be a motive for people to decide to work with you. We live in a selfish world and it only makes sense that if someone is to partner with you, they will also gain some benefits. At the end of the day, you need to think of your customers. If the partnerships do not match your clients' needs, then you must step back and say 'no'. Not all partnerships will be worth it in the end. So do not waste your time. You need to interview potential companies who want to work with you. You also need to be picky.

There have been instances where I wish I had not made myself so available for these opportunities. I should have been better at establishing whether their interest was casual or serious before spending too much time on them.

I should have set up a phone call with them first and then, if there was any further interest, fixed up a date to meet rather than just setting up the meeting straight away. This would have enabled me to filter people who were the most serious and prioritise spending my time and efforts on them. Those who are casually interested are not necessarily a waste of your time, but you don't need to rush to see them nor tell them everything you do and offer.

Also, if someone representing a brands says to you that they're on a low budget, then make sure you research what their budget has already been spent on. That way you can work out whether the brand actually does have a high budget, but they just do not value you enough. Walk away.

# LESSON 28

**A**s I have said before, the success of any meeting lies in both sides being clear on what they want to get out of it. If a company approaches you, you need to read between their lines and figure out what they are looking to gain from working with you and what you will gain if you do. You must be careful that during the meeting both your time and their time is used in a way that is beneficial to both parties. You must try to figure out why they have actually approached you. What are they desperate to achieve? What obstacle do they have to overcome in order to make it beneficial for them? It is very satisfying to work all this out. With any brand you partner with, be as blunt as possible and ask them what problem they currently have and how much they want to grow. With this information you can decide on how much time you will offer them and how much this is going to cost you.

**A DREAM YOU DREAM ALONE**

**IS ONLY A DREAM.**

**A DREAM YOU DREAM**

**TOGETHER IS REALITY.**

**YOKO ONO**

# 29

## THE LONELY ENTREPRENEUR

Throughout the months of June and July 2018, I was really down, really disappointed in myself for not achieving my goals and disappointed that I had also not satisfied many of my members. It was all getting too much for me. I was alone. Those months were the only months, to date, where it felt miserable. I couldn't speak to anyone about it. I didn't want to speak to my family about it, nor did I really want to speak to friends about it. I just wanted to figure out what to do. I felt like I was waiting around far too long for things to happen, but at the end of the day, I was a one-woman show and all decisions were made by me. I realised that I couldn't do everything myself, and this ultimately affected everything to do with the business.

# NOTES

....................................................................

....................................................................

....................................................................

....................................................................

....................................................................

....................................................................

....................................................................

....................................................................

# LESSON 29

Don't go down a negative route, because no one, in my opinion, will put you back up. It has to come from you. Stay focused and feisty, greedy and energetic. Take a week break if you have to. I went cycling in France, which meant that realistically and physically, I couldn't even check my phone. If you are checking your phone on holiday, ensure it is only for a maximum of 30 minutes, or in the case of an emergency. Go and find a similar reason to do just that, ensuring that you also take enough mental breaks. Or if you need to speak to someone, find as much help as possible. There are business coaches available, mentors, consultants, friends, family, never feel like it's all on you. Don't feel guilty or worried about delegating, delegate work as much as possible to volunteers, interns, friends and family. Even outsource some of your own work to VAs (Virtual Assistants) who are trained and qualified to assist you.

**"**

OUR FATIGUE IS OFTEN

CAUSED NOT BY WORK,

BUT BY WORRY, FRUSTRATION

AND RESENTMENT.

**"**

DALE CARNEGIE

# 30

## THE END...
## WELL, NOT REALLY

had thought that by the time it came to September 2018, I would have reached the definition of success, grasped all opportunities and taken the whole of the student market. But actually my failure lied in my dependency on new pitches and potential new partnerships, which were proving so slow to develop. As time went on, days, weeks and even up to August, I hadn't heard back from the 'ever so keen' companies who had been desperate to partner with me. It was confusing, it was frustrating and actually very disappointing. I had no clue what was going on, why they were so slow. I eventually learnt that it doesn't matter if there are agreements or contracts signed, you cannot depend on anyone else to make anything happen. Why partner with a company promising to bring 20 different luxury brands on board, when you can just do it yourself? In the time I waited for results, I could have achieved a lot myself. From previous examples, I can tell you now I am a 'go-getter' so why suddenly delegate or think other ways would be better?

# NOTES

..............................................................

..............................................................

..............................................................

..............................................................

..............................................................

..............................................................

..............................................................

..............................................................

# LESSON 30

Always trust your own actions; never leave a project that you feel you depend on so much, to anyone else. Share the workload or responsibility with others in your team, but at the end of the day, it is your task, your goal.

**"**

SOMEONE IS SITTING IN THE

SHADE TODAY BECAUSE

SOMEONE PLANTED A TREE A

LONG TIME AGO.

**"**

WARREN BUFFETT

## 31

# NEARLY REACHING ONE
# YEAR SINCE THE RELAUNCH

What on earth am I doing? I asked myself at the beginning of August. I felt so lost that day, I had no idea what to do or how to develop the business. I felt that I had dug myself into a hole filled with ideas and concerns, potentials and risks. I felt so overwhelmed and I was so desperate for someone to just give me a nudge, a hint, something to put me back in my Aileen The Entrepreneur mode. I had enough mentors around to help me during these difficult times, but even their help wasn't clicking in.

I realised that although I am a big fan of networking and building connections, and had connected with so many people in the past three years, I had not really taken advantage of their knowledge. I then decided to go to my LinkedIn page and headed straight to the bottom of my inbox. I went all the way back to the people I had messaged or connected to years ago, and reviewed whether in all this time I should have made more effort. Well, as you can imagine, there were plenty of people on that list. This made me feel angry at myself for not building these potentially golden relationships. So I messaged a lot of people in my inbox, hoping that maybe a few would remember who I was.

To my surprise, a businessman who I met at a networking event came back to me and replied with so much enthusiasm, (literally with emojis) and said how I was such a nice girl three years ago, when we met, and he was very happy to help, and that he was free today for a call. I was relieved, so happy and so surprised. I called immediately and I wish I had somehow recorded the conversation, but he said how excited he was when he had met me in the early days of Luxury Student and how he was always eager to hear how everything was going. The conversation was a delight and we shared information, he shared useful contacts and he gave me very good tips. I said thank you so many times in that conversation because I was so utterly grateful. It was exactly what I needed to get me back on track.

# LESSON 31

Don't waste time feeling down or confused. Find help in any shape or form, even if you have to go through all the contacts in your phone, LinkedIn or Instagram – find someone to help or discuss your worries and goals. Sometimes it's nice to meet someone you haven't seen in a while. It gives you an outsider or 'bigger-picture' approach as you will be describing things without so much detail. Also, any contact is a good contact. One day you can help them.

**"**

I STRONGLY BELIEVE IF YOU

WORK HARD, WHATEVER YOU

WANT, IT WILL COME TO YOU.

I KNOW THAT'S EASIER SAID

THAN DONE BUT KEEP TRYING.

**"**

BEYONCÉ

# 32

## MY BUSINESS WORKS, NOW CAN I RELAX?

'm 26, have a concept that finally works, a market that accepts it and brands who support it. It is satisfying to say that after what felt like a very long and frustrating time, there is finally potential. I have an exciting website that I can do anything with. This means I can be open-minded, and open to different revenue streams in the future. Those revenue streams that didn't really work in the beginning, have now finally had a chance to blossom. It's easy for me to say I have made it, but actually I haven't. There are still times where we really do muck up, from customer service to sales or PR and even my own personal brand. Remember that investment that I didn't need in the beginning? Well, I actually do need it now. Again, plans, vision, thoughts change on a daily basis. It has to because it has to suit the current situation.

I wake up at 8am, go through all the social media and any updates. 8:30am is coffee and email updates with my PR agency. 9am I'm either heading to the office or a venue, or sometimes I stay at home to just crack on with emails. I often have meetings throughout the day – with new brand partnerships, brand ambassadors, interns and sometimes I try to fit in a meeting with new members as well. I also have daily meetings with a mentor or friend, this gives me a break because it forces me to be myself a bit and not just my brand.

Then back to emails, usually checking social media private messages, as usually if people can't get hold of me in emails, they hint to me on messages that they need a reply. Then, while most people go home, I brainstorm more ideas to partner with more brands and find new ways to grow the business.

At some point, I either go to host an event with a brand or I go home. En route I'll buy some food for dinner, usually having nothing in the fridge. Then, to treat myself, I watch a TV series in PJs and then meditate.

# LESSON 32

If you think that having a small slice of success means you can relax, then you certainly have got it wrong. You will never relax. In fact, it will probably get as crazy for you as it does for me and any entrepreneur. But make sure it is good stress. It sounds odd, but make sure that in these hectic days, you know at the back of your mind that it's fun and it's good for you. I love what I am doing. I wouldn't replace it with anything else or take back my decision to start this business. To be honest, there are times where I wish I could just switch off from it, but, ultimately, knowing that any good that comes out of this business is from my hard work is the most valuable and exciting feeling!

**"**

YOU GET ONE LIFE.

I'M GOING TO EMBRACE MINE.

**"**

KEVIN HART

# 33

## INVEST IN YOURSELF AND YOUR FUTURE!

I t's only right to end this book with a chapter about you! I have always thought very highly of myself, because at school I was a drama and musical performer, so I already had a lot of confidence by the time I reached university. I was never nervous to start conversations; in fact, I loved being the entertainer. I was very opinionated and knew what I liked and what I didn't like. I was a people pleaser, but I also had standards. The moral of the story is that I already valued myself greatly, compared to many people around me. When I started The Luxury Student, even as a blog, I just knew it was going to go far and I knew that I was vital to its success. I, as a brand, had to make sure that I represented myself and the business.

# NOTES

........................................................

........................................................

........................................................

........................................................

........................................................

........................................................

........................................................

........................................................

# LESSON 33

**M**y last lesson for you is to at least invest in your website domain. Buy the domain, even if you don't have the confidence in the business now. My secret first step before even thinking of starting my business, was to invest in buying aileengilani.com, plus all the other domains that I could think of that linked to my name. I did this because at the time I thought entrepreneurs were like celebrities! This is how exciting I thought running a business was, it still is. I didn't use all of the domains, but I have them and I can use them one day to work on my own personal blog or even run another business with this name. The point is, you will never know what will happen in the near future or just how successful you may be. There may be a time when people will be desperate to know who you are. Be confident that your life will be a success!

# CONNECT

I f you're interested in being part of the community of STUDENT TO ENTREPRENEUR then follow us @luxurystudententrepreneur

I f you're a luxury lover, join the membership to gain access to all luxury benefits and add the code LUXURYBOOK to receive a gift from us!

I f you liked the book and wish to have more help from me, then please join my new Start-up Mentoring Programme where you will receive a fun start-up branding pack and workshop held by The Luxury Student Team! www.luxurystudent.com/mentor

@facebook.com/theluxurystudent

Instagram @theluxurystudent

Twitter @luxstudent

LinkedIn Aileen Gilani

@luxurystudententrepreneur

www.luxurystudent.com